FREEDOM FORCES

★ THE CIA AND FBI: ★

TOP SECRET

Sneed B. Collard III

Rourke
Educational Media
rourkeeducationalmedia.com

www.rourkeeducationalmedia.com

PHOTO CREDITS: Cover: Background © Bruce Rolff, agent © Peter Kim, Top Secret logo © james weston; Title Page © Background © Bruce Rolff, Top Secret logo © james weston; back cover and title page: flag © SFerdon; Pages 4/5 © U.S. Federal Government/FEMA, and Michael Foran Page 6 courtesy of Library Of Congress; Page 7: FBI; Page 8 Bonnie and Clyde: FBI, Kennedy courtesy of the Library of Congress; Page 9 courtesy of The Hoover Library of Congress; Pages 10-12 courtesy of the FBI; background photo page 12-13 © Semisatch; Pages 14/15 Berlin Wall © Alicar; Page 15 map © Mosedschurte, Pages 16/17 © CIA, Library of Congress, Semhur; Pages 18 Castro courtesy of Library of Congress, Map © AridOcean; Page 19 map © Tupungato, military photo courtesy U.S. Army; Pages 20/21 courtesy of U.S. Government, except art of folders © McVectors Pages 22/23 courtesy of CIA Pages 24 courtesy of Voice of America; Page 25 courtesy U.S. Air Force photo/Lt Col Leslie Pratt; Pages 26/27 © FBI, Leah-Anne Thompson, EpicFlame; Pages 28 courtesy of Library of Congress; Page 29 U.S. Federal Government/FEMA

Edited by Precious McKenzie

Designed and Produced by Blue Door Publishing, FL

Library of Congress Cataloging-in-Publication Data

The CIA and FBI: Top Secret / Sneed B. Collard III
  p. cm. -- (Freedom Forces)
  ISBN 978-1-62169-925-5 (hard cover) (alk. paper)
  ISBN 978-1-62169-820-3 (soft cover)
  ISBN 978-1-62717-029-1 (e-book)
Library of Congress Control Number: 2013938877

Rourke Educational Media
Printed in the United States of America,
North Mankato, Minnesota

Also Available as:
ROURKE'S e-Books

Rourke
Educational Media
rourkeeducationalmedia.com
customerservice@rourkeeducationalmedia.com
PO Box 643328 Vero Beach, Florida 32964

TABLE OF CONTENTS

CHAPTER ONE
DEVASTATION

The failure of the United States to prevent the September 11th, 2001, attacks on the World Trade Center and the Pentagon shook the United States intelligence community. Every intelligence organization shared blame for the disaster that claimed almost 3,000 lives on American soil. Two agencies stood out, however: the **FBI**, or Federal Bureau of Investigation, and the **CIA**, the Central Intelligence Agency. The terrorists' 9/11 plans slipped by both organizations. Today, the agencies are dedicated to making sure nothing like 9/11 ever happens again.

Ground Zero in New York City and the Pentagon in Washington D.C. will forever be remembered as a place where dedicated emergency workers risked their lives saving people and fighting the ferocious fires.

5

The FBI is the nation's oldest intelligence agency. Its primary objectives are to protect American citizens and uphold the laws of the United States. Specifically, the FBI seeks to prevent terrorist attacks, protect against foreign spies, and stop dangerous computer hacking. The FBI is also charged with upholding **civil rights**, and investigating both violent and **white-collar crime**. To perform these, and other objectives, it has to collect vast amounts of information, both here in the United States and overseas. Unlike the CIA, the FBI also has the job of law enforcement. Once a crime is detected, FBI agents have the power to make arrests and prosecute accused criminals.

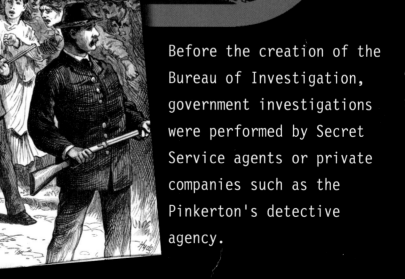

Before the creation of the Bureau of Investigation, government investigations were performed by Secret Service agents or private companies such as the Pinkerton's detective agency.

Nearly 18 million background checks are performed each year by the FBI. The FBI maintains supercomputing resources with the ability to decrypt secure media in one day!

The FBI began simply as the Bureau of Investigation in 1908. The Department of Justice hired a small number of agents to investigate **federal** crimes. These were crimes that involved our national government, or crimes that crossed state lines.

Bonnie and Clyde were well-known American outlaws, robbers, and criminals.

During World Wars I and II, Bureau agents combated foreign spies and those who wanted to sabotage American industries. During **Prohibition**, when alcohol was made illegal, agents pursued famous mobsters such as Al Capone, and Bonnie and Clyde. Since then, FBI agents have investigated everything from the assassination of President John F. Kennedy to the rampages of serial killers.

The 35th President of the United States, John F. Kennedy, was fatally shot while traveling with his wife in a presidential motorcade.

One man, more than any other, influenced the evolution of the FBI. J. Edgar Hoover assumed control of the FBI in 1924 at the age of 29, and remained director until he died in 1972. Under Hoover, the FBI underwent extraordinary growth. Its agents became top-notch professionals through rigorous selection and training. Many people accused Hoover of abusing his power, however. Hoover compiled secret files on many Americans including the Kennedys and Martin Luther King, Jr. Most Americans feared Hoover. During the 1950s and 1960s, Hoover's hatred of communists led him to ignore organized crime and try to undermine the Civil Rights movement.

J. Edgar Hoover

The FBI also have canine agents! These explosives detection canines can pick up about 19,000 different explosive combinations.

FEDERAL BUREAU OF INVESTIGATION

SWAT team members undergo extensive training regimens in weapons and tactical scenarios. An FBI SWAT can have up to 42 members.

CHAPTER THREE CRIME AND TERROR TODAY

Since 9/11, however, fighting terror has vaulted to the top of the FBI's priority list. By late 2012, the FBI employed 36,074 people, including 13,913 **special agents**. Many of these agents focus on investigating possible terrorist activities here in the United States and overseas. To do this, they use a variety of tools. They interview suspects and witnesses. They collect and compare fingerprints and **DNA** of possible suspects. They use wiretaps to record phone conversations, and much, much more.

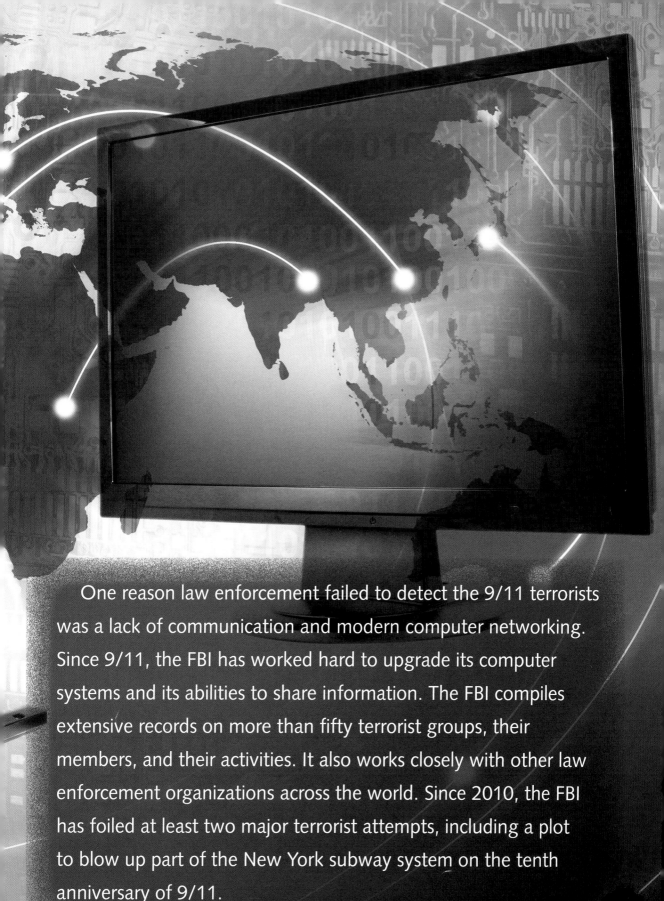

One reason law enforcement failed to detect the 9/11 terrorists was a lack of communication and modern computer networking. Since 9/11, the FBI has worked hard to upgrade its computer systems and its abilities to share information. The FBI compiles extensive records on more than fifty terrorist groups, their members, and their activities. It also works closely with other law enforcement organizations across the world. Since 2010, the FBI has foiled at least two major terrorist attempts, including a plot to blow up part of the New York subway system on the tenth anniversary of 9/11.

The Berlin Wall served as a barrier that completely cut off West Berlin from surrounding East Germany and East Berlin. The barrier included guard towers that contained anti-vehicle trenches and other defenses.

CHAPTER FOUR

THE BIRTH OF THE CIA

President Harry S. Truman signed the law creating the Central Intelligence Agency in 1947. After World War II, many government leaders, along with the military, recognized the need to build a permanent intelligence organization. The U.S. especially wanted to track the activities of foreign countries, including the new superpowers China and the Soviet Union. Unlike the FBI, the CIA's job did not involve enforcing laws. Its mission was simple: collect information and spy on the enemy.

The CIA was created at the dawn of the **Cold War.** The Soviet Union and China were both spreading Communism to other nations and building nuclear weapons. Americans worried that they might soon fight a nuclear war with either or both nations.

UNITED STATES

SOVIET UNION

CHINA

The idea of the CIA was straight out of a James Bond movie. The goal? Create and maintain a network of spies around the world that would report back to Washington, D.C. CIA agents would gather information and hire informants, especially behind the **Iron Curtain**, inside the Soviet Union and its allies. Sometimes, CIA agents would plan secret missions to steal information, kill other spies, and overthrow foreign leaders.

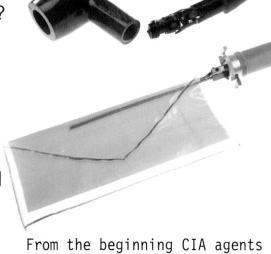

From the beginning CIA agents have had some pretty cool gadgets including a radio transmitter hidden inside a pipe and a letter opener that doesn't rip envelopes.

In the world of spies, a mole, or informant, is an agent who trades or sells information to outside governments.

Aldrich Ames, a former CIA officer was convicted of spying and selling data to the Soviet Union and Russia. This CIA mole was sentenced to life imprisonment by the United States Department of Justice on February 22, 1994.

Aldrich Ames

Operation Paperclip was the Office of Strategic Services program used to recruit the scientists of Nazi Germany for employment by the United States in the aftermath of World War II. The project's operational name derived from the paperclips used to attach the scientists' new political personae to their U.S. Government Scientist personnel files.

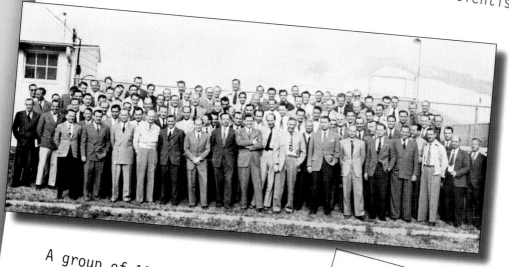

A group of 104 German rocket scientists worked to develop the V-2 Rocket in 1946. This single stage ballistic missile could reach a speed of 3,580 mph (5,761 kph).

CHAPTER FIVE A ROCKY ROAD

Unfortunately, the CIA struggled to achieve its goals. Agents from other governments often knew who CIA agents were and fed them false information. Incorrect CIA information led to the failed Bay of Pigs invasion of Cuba in April 1961.

UNITED STATES

Cuba

Fidel Castro in 1959

The Bay of Pigs invasion was an attempt to oust Cuba's leader Fidel Castro. Castro was an ally of the Soviet Union and, because of this, posed a danger to the United States. The CIA trained and organized a small group of former Cubans to attack Cuba to try to overthrow the government. Castro's forces were waiting for them. More than 1,200 of the invaders were captured and many of them killed.

Four decades later, the CIA claimed that Iraq possessed Weapons of Mass Destruction, or WMDs. No WMDs were ever found, but that bad information propelled the United States into the war and occupation of Iraq. In cases where CIA information was accurate, politicians and the military sometimes ignored it, with terrible consequences.

The invasion of Iraq consisted of 21 days of major combat operations. U.S. Army M1A1 Abrams tanks and their crews pose in the front of the *Hands of Victory* monument at Baghdad's Ceremony Square.

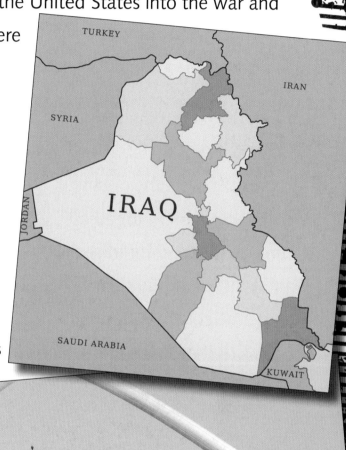

19

The CIA's and FBI's biggest disaster, however, was 9/11. Before the attacks, the CIA had already been tracking Osama bin Laden and Al Qaeda. The FBI also possessed key information about the terrorists who carried out the attacks. Unfortunately, neither agency put the information together in time to prevent the tragedy. Part of the blame lay with

President George W. Bush

President George W. Bush and his staff, which ignored warnings by the CIA that some kind of terrorist attack would soon happen.

Osama Bin Laden

The CIA's effort to determine the location of Osama Bin Laden eventually resulted in the Abbottabad operation. This operation began with a fragment of information unearthed in 2002, resulting in years of investigation until his assassination in 2011.

As a result of the attack, Congress decided to reorganize the U.S. intelligence community. In 2004, Congress ordered that the CIA, the FBI, and fifteen other agencies begin reporting to the new Office of the Director of National Intelligence, or DNI.

The goal of DNI is to make sure that key intelligence information is shared, analyzed, and communicated to the President of the United States.

The CIA, FBI, and fifteen other agencies work both independently and collaboratively to conduct foreign relations and national security activities. The other fifteen agencies include:

Air Force Intelligence
Department of the Treasury
Army Intelligence
Drug Enforcement Administration
Bureau of Intelligence and Research
Coast Guard Intelligence
Marine Corps Intelligence
Defense Intelligence Agency
National Geospatial-Intelligence Agency
Department of Energy
National Reconnaissance Office
Department of Homeland Security
National Security Agency
Department of State
Navy Intelligence

The CIA headquarters are located in McLean, Virginia. It provides intelligence products to the President, the National Security Council, Congress, and other government agencies.

The number of people working for the CIA and the amount of money it spends are both **classified**. Estimates are that the CIA employs between 100,000 and 200,000 people and has a budget exceeding $40 billion per year.

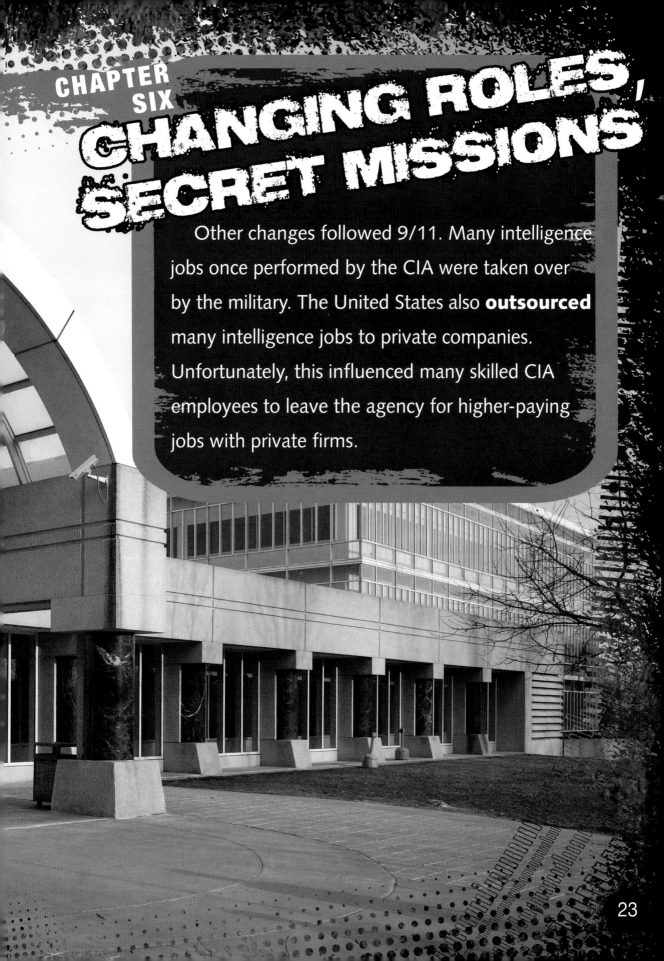

CHAPTER SIX
CHANGING ROLES, SECRET MISSIONS

Other changes followed 9/11. Many intelligence jobs once performed by the CIA were taken over by the military. The United States also **outsourced** many intelligence jobs to private companies. Unfortunately, this influenced many skilled CIA employees to leave the agency for higher-paying jobs with private firms.

Nonetheless, the CIA, like the FBI, has continued to focus its efforts on the War on Terror. CIA agents have played critical roles in preparing for the invasions of Afghanistan and Iraq. They have located key terrorists, including Osama bin Laden. The CIA has also conducted its own assassinations of terrorists using armed **drones**. Many other CIA operations remain top secret, but there's no doubt that CIA agents are currently operating in every country on Earth, working to keep America safe.

These bombed vehicles were a result of the street fighting that occurred in Aleppo, Syria in October, 2012. The CIA operated along the Turkish-Syrian border investigating rebel groups,developing supply routes, and giving aid.

MQ-1 Predators are operated from the ground by a three-man crew. Each Predator air vehicle can be disassembled into six main components and loaded into a container nicknamed the *coffin*.

INTELLIGENCE CAREERS

As the world continues to change, the roles of the FBI and CIA will continue to change with it. Both agencies offer a huge range of job opportunities. The FBI offers jobs to highly qualified college graduates in law enforcement, foreign languages, criminal investigation, and many other careers. The CIA hires scientists, engineers, computer specialists, spies, and many other professionals. Maybe a top secret career with the FBI or CIA is for you!

Agent in training

TO LEARN MORE ABOUT EXCITING CAREERS WITH THE FBI OR CIA, EXPLORE THE FOLLOWING WEBSITES:

FBI Careers Website:
https://www.fbijobs.gov/index.asp

CIA Careers Website:
https://www.cia.gov/careers/opportunities/index.html

Scientist

Sign language interpreter

Bomb technicians' vehicle

TIMELINE

1908:
The Bureau of Investigation created

1928:
Hoover establishes first formal training course for new agents

1935:
The Bureau of Investigation renamed the Federal Bureau of Investigation

1924:
J. Edgar Hoover appointed Director of the Bureau of Investigation

1920s and 30s:
FBI successfully puts many high-profile gangsters behind bars

1936–1945 World War II era:
FBI focuses on threats from foreign nations, spies, and sabotage

1947:
Central Intelligence Agency formed from World War II Office of Strategic Services

1970s-1990s:
CIA rocked by scandals that it engaged in a wide range of illegal activities

2004:
CIA and FBI begin reporting to the Director of National Intelligence

1953-1966
Early Cold War:
CIA works with military to spy on the Soviet Union and other hostile nations

2001:
CIA and FBI fail to uncover and stop attacks on the Pentagon and World Trade Center

2001-present:
CIA operations lead to assassination of many top terrorists, including Osama bin Laden; FBI thwarts major U.S. terrorist attacks

SHOW WHAT YOU KNOW

1. Why was the FBI created?
2. Why was the CIA created?
3. Explain jobs that the FBI performs.
4. Explain jobs that the CIA performs.
5. Since 9/11, how have the CIA and FBI changed?

GLOSSARY

CIA (C I A): Central Intelligence Agency

civil rights (SI-vul rites): the freedoms, rights, and privileges of private citizens

classified (KLASS-uh-fide): secret and not available for the public to see

Cold War (kold wore): the build up of weapons and tensions between the United States and the former Soviet Union from the 1950s into the 1980s

DNA (D N A): genetic information contained in a person's cells that can be used to identify a person or where a person has been

drones (dronz): unmanned aircraft, often equipped with weapons systems

FBI (F B I): Federal Bureau of Investigation

federal (FED-ur-ul): having to do with the national government, as opposed to state or local governments

Iron Curtain (EYE-urn Kur-ten): beyond the borders of the former Soviet Union and its allies

outsourced (OWT-sorst): having to do with a job given to a private company

Prohibition (PRO-hi-BI-shun): the years from 1920 to 1933 during which the production, sale, and transportation of most alcoholic beverages were illegal in the United States

special agents (SPE-shul A-jents): agents charged with investigating crimes and making arrests

white-collar crime (WITE col-UHR CRIME): non-violent crime that usually involves fraud or theft from banks, companies, and individuals by manipulating information

Index

Websites to Visit

http://www.fbi.gov/

http://www.fbi.gov/fun-games/kids/

https://www.cia.gov/kids-page/index.html

About the Author

Sneed B. Collard III has written more than 65 books for young people including the award-winning books *Science Warriors—The Battle Against Invasive Species*, *Pocket Babies and Other Amazing Marsupials*, and *The World Famous Miles City Bucking Horse Sale*. His popular novels include *Dog Sense, Hangman's Gold, and Cartwheel—A Sequel to Double Eagle*. Watch book trailers for Sneed's books on his YouTube channel, and learn more about him at www.sneedbcollardiii.com.

Meet The Author!
www.meetREMauthors.com